Dedicated To:
Nativity Catholic School
Leawood, Kansas

Written By: Abigail Gartland

Hello, my name is St. George!

I was born in Turkey in the year 200!

The legend of my story starts with when I was young.

When I was a boy, I lived by a lake.

I loved the lake, but there was one HUGE problem!

There was a dragon that lived in the lake!

Everyone was very scared of the dragon.

The dragon stayed happy if he was allowed to keep two sheep each day.

But ... then the dragon not only wanted to keep the two sheep, he also wanted a child!

One day, the dragon wanted to take the king's daughter to be his child.

When I heard about this, I decided to save the king's daughter.

I slayed the dragon, and he fell into the water.

I saved the king's daughter!

I knew the whole time that God was with me.

I am the patron saint of knights and being brave!

Do you want to be more like me?

You can celebrate my feast day with me on April 23rd.

I pray for you every day of your life.

St. George, Pray for us!

Copyright:

Clipart: © PentoolPixie © LimeandKiwiDesigns
Licensed purchased: 1/10/2024

About the Author

Abigail Gartland

I love the saints and I love my faith. The idea for sharing the stories of the saints with little ones came when my dear friends were expecting their first baby. I wanted to create something as unique and special as our friendship. Each book is dedicated to very special people and groups who have enriched my faith in different ways. I am blessed to write these stories and appreciate the unending support of my family and friends. When I am not writing, I am a middle school teacher. I hope you enjoy these stories. I pray for each and every person who opens one of my books to learn more about the saints.

Abbie

www.ingramcontent.com/pod-product-compliance
Lightning Source LLC
LaVergne TN
LVHW051043070526
838201LV00067B/4898